The College De-Stress Handbook

Keeping Cool Under Pressure From the Inside Out

Jeff Goelitz
Robert A. Rees, Ph.D.

INSTITUTE OF HEARTMATH®
Connecting Hearts and Minds

Institute of HeartMath
14700 West Park Avenue
Boulder Creek, California, 95006 USA

www.heartmath.org

Phone: (831) 338-8500
email: info@heartmath.org

Contributing Editor: Rollin McCraty, Ph.D.

Cartoon Illustrator: Jett Atwood

*Most of the names of the students and their college institutions used in this book
have either been changed or deleted to protect their identities.*

Library of Congress Cataloging-in-Publication Data
Goelitz, Jeff; Rees, Robert A.
ISBN 9780983952008
1. Self-Help Techniques 2. Mind and Body
10 9 8 7 6 5 4 3 2 1 First Edition 2011

Comments from College Professionals

"I have trained hundreds of students in HeartMath's stress-reducing techniques. Scientific studies have shown that these easy-to-learn tools neutralize the interference of emotion on thought. My students report clear thinking in pressure-packed situations such as test-taking, learning math, public speaking and passing national registry exams. Many have reported life-changing experiences. I heartily recommend this book as a practical handbook for students at all colleges to experience what I've witnessed in students here and in my own life."

—*John Coles, Ph.D., professor of psychology, Truckee Meadows Community College, Reno, Nev.*

"As part of our *Brain, Affect and Education* concentration, college and university students study the effects of the autonomic nervous system (ANS) balance and imbalance. With HeartMath technology and techniques to help them, they learn to strategically control ANS for positive benefits to immunity, respiration, digestion, cardiac function and cognitive processing – all of which impact learning. College students will appreciate this book, but so will teachers who want to create positive learning environments."

—*Linda Caviness, Ph.D., curriculum and instruction chair, school of education, La Sierra University*

"Over the last 8 years, I have used HeartMath programs and technologies to help hundreds of my students. Students report reductions in stress and test anxiety while improving their decision-making and relationships. Ultimately, they are training the frontal cortex part of their brains to think more clearly and gain greater perspective on what is important in daily life."

—*Ron Leslie, Ph.D., professor of psychology, University of Cincinnati at Clermont, Batavia, Ohio*

"Research in positive psychology has revealed a strong association between positive emotional states and significant mental and physical health benefits. In addition, positive emotions can enhance performance in academics, work, sports, creative pursuits, and social interactions. The simple techniques discussed in this book are capable of producing an almost instantaneous shift to a positive emotional state. With regular practice, benefits can be achieved even in the face of stressful events."

—*Henry J. Kahn, M.D., professor of clinical medicine,*
University of California, San Francisco

"Stress causes too many students to perform below their abilities. The Learning Center of the University of Alaska Southeast currently offers HeartMath tools to lower stress and improve performance. We are eager to share this new book with our student body to further help them in their quest for academic success."

—*Hildegard Sellner, Ph.D., learning center director,*
University of Alaska Southeast, Juneau

"I heartily recommend this book as a practical guide to help college students become more emotionally fit, manage their stress levels, optimize performance in high stakes situations, and cope more successfully with the current demands of professional and college life. I teach these techniques to my undergraduate and graduate university students in programs that range from Education to Emergency Services Administration. They report success in using the techniques both on the job and in their academic activities."

—*Joanne Tortorici Luna, Ph.D., licensed psychologist, professor advanced studies*
in education and counseling, California State University, Long Beach

"I enthusiastically recommend this book. It will help students lessen their stress while building greater resilience in the face of challenges and complexities in college life."

—*Catherine Augustine, Ph.D., academic counselor, Penn State University*

Table of Contents

Chapter 1

Navigating the College Maze

For many students, college can be like walking through a maze. There are a bewildering number of choices to make and things to do, and students are pulled and pressured from all directions. Although there are signposts to guide you through these complex paths toward the final prize, graduation and a degree, you must constantly navigate your way, and this requires the ability to weigh options and decide which choices to make at every turn.

Everyone says you get as much out of college as you put into it. It can be one of the richest and most memorable times of your life, but it also can be one of the most challenging and stressful. How well you manage your stress can make all the difference in the quality of your college experience.

There is a joke about a college student proudly showing off his new apartment to friends.

"What is the big brass gong and hammer for?" a friend asks.

"That is the talking clock," the student replies.

"Talking clock? What do you mean?"

"Watch this," the student says as he proceeds to give the gong an ear-shattering bang with the hammer.

Suddenly, someone screams from the other side of the wall, "Knock it off, you idiot! It's two o'clock in the morning!"

Besides being kept up late by the occasional student reveler, an all-nighter for a research paper or tending to a sick child at home, there are many other reasons why you might be experiencing stress in college – whether you are a freshman in a dorm, a junior living off campus with friends, or a married student commuting to and from school.

As you likely have discovered, academic work can be very challenging, and the competition to earn top grades can be fierce. In addition, many students must work part time or take out large loans to pay for college. Also, while you are figuring out your major and focusing on a career choice, you know that when you graduate you likely will be entering a tough job market and facing an uncertain economic future. Along with these big decisions, you also will have to make a number of other important ones about managing your time, money and relationships – all of which can add to your stress.

Only some of the factors that make college a high-stress environment are within your control. The good news is that those within your control can help you cope with those that are not.

One of the main things you can control is your knowledge – knowledge about the nature of stress, how it affects you and what you can do about it, so you can live a more balanced life with less stress.

The purpose of this book is to teach you exactly that – *how to live a more balanced life with less stress.*

What is Stress?

According to the American Institute of Stress, there is no definition of stress on which everyone agrees, but the following generally describe how most of us experience it:

- "A state of extreme difficulty, pressure, or strain."[1]
- "The body's reaction to a change that requires a physical, mental or emotional adjustment or response."[2]
- "Your body's way of responding to any kind of demand."[3]

Another way of putting it is that we experience stress when we have too much to do and not enough time to do it in. We also can think of stress as "emotional unease"– the feeling that something is out of sync, but you probably don't need a definition of stress to tell you how it feels.

Emotions we tend to associate with stress are *anger, frustration, and anxiety* – the sense that things are spinning out of control. Ever feel that way? You are not alone.

Sources of Stress for College Students

Some students are under so much stress they get sick or drop out of college. *Here, according to various surveys, are some of the main reasons students drop out of college.*[4]

- A sense of not belonging, feeling isolated and homesick
- Academically unprepared
- Financial problems
- Personal or family issues
- Academic overload and falling behind
- Too much fun at the expense of classes and grades

- Inadequate guidance
- Work
- Relocation

What all of these stressors have in common is that they lead to stressful or energy-draining perceptions and emotions. If some of them apply to you, you are typical of the average college student. You probably feel, as most students do, the need to find more balance and resilience to counter the effects of stress. Some may be like the ostrich and bury their heads in the sand, hoping the problem will go away, but it won't, of course. Generally, stress only goes away when we do something about it.

How Stress Shows Up Differently for Everyone

Most people experience stressful emotions in specific situations: running out of money partway through the semester, trying to balance personal and family needs, preparing for a midterm or breaking up with someone they like a lot. For many people, stress can manifest itself with physical symptoms such as headaches or stomachaches.

People can respond differently to the same event or challenge. One person who receives an unexpected poor grade can become angry or depressed, while someone else could see this as a challenge to do better, without becoming angry or depressed.

Here are some student comments about college:

- "The first few weeks of college, I felt free as a bird! I didn't have my parents looking over my shoulder every day. Unfortunately, even though I was free to make lots of choices, I didn't always choose well. I partied and played too much and got way behind in a couple of classes. Getting caught up has been very stressful, which hasn't felt good. I'm hoping I've learned my lesson and won't get in such deep trouble next semester."

- "I really like going to school two nights a week because it means I'm not home taking care of kids every single night. My husband comes home from work and I pass the parent baton to him and am out the door. Unfortunately, the next day I feel like Cinderella the day after the ball. Juggling school with shopping, cooking, laundry and taking care of kids has really added a lot of stress to my life, but I love being a student!"

- "I'm a sophomore at a small Ivy League college. I chose this school because of its academic reputation, but I often feel like a fish out of water. My classmates seem to have more money than I do, and they tend to be cliquish. I've had a hard time finding friends and am wondering if I made the right choice in coming here. I'd consider dropping out, but I don't want to disappoint my parents, especially with the sacrifices they are making to send me here. Some nights, I can't sleep because I'm thinking about it so much."

- "I'm from Chicago and so I thought it would be a good idea to go to a small Midwestern college. As much as I like watching corn grow, I really miss the hustle and bustle of the city. I'm trying to adjust and am committed to finishing out my first year, but I'm not sure I'm coming back next year. Maybe by June I will get used to having one theater in town, two fast-food restaurants, and a million ears of corn!"

Are You a Stress Statistic?

Although the experience of stressful feelings is unique and subjective for each individual, what is abundantly clear is that stress is pervasive. Nearly half (48 percent) of Americans feel their stress has increased over the past five years, and one-third feel they are living with extreme stress. Stress causes more than half of Americans to have conflicts with people close to them.[5]

The American Institute of Stress estimates that 75 percent to 90 percent of visits to primary-care physicians are for stress-related complaints.[6]

It can be worse for college students. Eighty-five percent of college students surveyed in an *Associated Press-mtvU poll* reported feeling stressed daily.[7] Worries about grades, schoolwork, money and relationships were the biggest issues. Forty-two percent said they had felt depressed or hopeless several days during the previous two weeks.[8] "Undergrads are overwhelmed and overcommitted," said Terry Wilson, director of health promotion and wellness at the University of Missouri Student Health Center. "We encourage students to get involved, but some join too many organizations. Some work on top of that. While we recommend a 12-hour course load, some students take 15, which is usually too much. With study, activities and work, many get overloaded quickly."

- "I feel really stressed," said Wendy Johnson, a senior finance and economics major at California State University, Fullerton. Johnson is taking 12 credit hours, so, including study time, she typically spends up to 35 hours a week on academics. She also works 20 to 30 hours per week at Target. "It doesn't seem like I have any free time. I get worried that I'm not going to finish projects, so I start to cut corners, which makes me stress even more."

- "Everything is being piled on at once," Michigan State University junior David Sherry said. "You just get really agitated and anxious. Then you start procrastinating, and it all piles up."

- "I'm working on getting my certificate in auto mechanics," said David Gonzales, a student at a technical institute in Virginia. "Unfortunately, since I'm married and have a kid, I have to work part time while going to school. I drink a lot of coffee and an occasional energy drink, and on weekends I sort of collapse. My blood pressure is too high, but I try not to think about it too much. My wife says I should slow down, but I don't think she understands how hard that is for me."

Whether or not you were in college in recent years, you likely would have experienced more stressful feelings than normal simply because of things such as the economy, political conflict, global unrest and climate change, to name only a few of the factors that can make life more uncertain, unpredictable and more stressful.

Because it is so widespread, stress can be contagious. Often, other people's drama, whether in the home, dorm, classroom, workplace, out on the highway, or even in social media like Facebook, increases our own stress load. We all broadcast our stress through attitudes, reactions, language and even subtle, nonverbal communication. Some people are so stressed they feel they don't have time to deal with it. Psychologists tell us that if we don't learn to regulate our stressful emotions, they will regulate us.

You know you're too stressed when...

- You tell your professor, "I haven't lost my mind. It's backed up on a thumb drive somewhere."

- The dean has your cellphone number on speed dial.

- Your cat is on Valium.

- You wake up in the library in your pajamas.

- People have trouble understanding you because you speak through clenched teeth.

- You don't have time to wait for the microwave to cook your 20-second snack.

- Conflicts with your roommate are mediated by law enforcement officials.

- Starbucks gives you industrial rates.

- You eat a package of Doritos at every meal.[9]

Stress is the Body's Warning Signal

It's easy to forget that stress is one of your body's warning signals that something is out of whack. If you ignore those signals, especially your emotions, you could become so accustomed to the stimulation of stress, ongoing tension and strain that stress can start to seem normal. When a lot of people in a particular environment are stressed, they can create a climate that makes it more difficult for any one person to see his or her own stress clearly.

"When you have a whole culture pushing high performance, stress can be so pervasive among students, professors, and support staff, that sometimes people don't want to admit it or address it," said Henry J. Kahn, M.D., director of student health and counseling services at the University of California, San Francisco. "I see many students who experience numerous symptoms of stress like headaches, dizziness, low energy, insomnia, eating disorders, and lack of concentration, but they don't always associate those symptoms with stress."

Stress can create a dynamic or creative challenge for some people if they approach it positively and don't let it get out of balance. For most of us, however, too much stress creates overload, causing our clarity and creativity to decline, and it creates a feeling of disconnection from ourselves and others. When this happens, we experience stress overload as aches and pains, negative attitudes, circular thinking, troubled relationships and a sense that things are getting out of control.

Where You First Experience Stress

You first experience stress in your feeling world. This is the space within you where you register feelings and moods. There is a lot of information contained in your feeling world, just as there is in your mind and body, and this information can be very useful if you know how to read your feelings. If you don't know how to read them, your feelings of tension, irritation and worry can escalate into stronger emotions of frustration, anxiety or anger. Finally, you end up overloaded and exhausted, and you accumulate stress when you carry around distressing feelings without resolving them.

People have difficulty acknowledging their feelings in our society. If your emotions are managing you, rather than you managing them, you may fear that others will judge you. If you're like most college students, you don't like to admit you're hurting or feeling bad, that emotions are running you ragged, or that you feel a slow burn inside. You'd rather ignore such feelings, hide or suppress them, or take them out on others.

When these stress-producing emotions are not managed, the feelings build up and are vented as judgments, projections or blame. If you can't find relief, you may blow up, want to go hide under the covers or become immobile like a deer staring into headlights. This is what's called the "fight, flight or freeze" response. Stress switches on brain circuits and hormones that prepare the body to protect itself in situations you might perceive as unsafe or threatening.

The problem is, this low-level survival mechanism in the brain can get activated by everyday situations that are challenging but not life threatening – an argument with a friend, a traffic jam, a looming term paper – until your mind, emotions and body are in stress overload. This stress response spills over into academic work. Students reported in a national survey that stress affected their academic performance more than any other single factor.[10]

It doesn't have to be this way. This handbook will show you how you can significantly reduce your stress and improve your academic performance at the same time.

Questions to Ponder

1. Everyone experiences stress uniquely. How do you experience it – physically, mentally and emotionally?

2. Do you feel comfortable talking about your stressful feelings with friends, family or others? Why or why not?

3. Identify which of your responses to stress are healthy and which are unhealthy.

4. Which of the responses of your fellow students are healthy and which are unhealthy?

5. How much do other people's stress and drama affect you?

Chapter 2

How the Heart, Brain and Body Affect Performance

This chapter contains basic information about how your brain and body respond to stress. On the surface, this topic might seem dry and boring but in truth this information can be extremely valuable to you, especially if you are motivated to improve your performance in areas like test-taking, decision-making, social relations and problem-solving.

To begin with, this information will help you understand some of the physiological processes that influence your thoughts and emotions and directly affect the areas in your brain involved in learning, memory and analytical thinking. It explains what goes on in your brain and nervous system when you experience either a stressful or positive emotion and how each affects your cognitive functioning. Understanding these physiological processes will help you become more aware of the signs of stress so you can begin managing your normal stress response more effectively. When you learn how different thoughts and emotions are affecting your physiology, you also will begin to understand which of your actions and attitudes renew your energy and which of them deplete it.

Imagine for a moment that you just had a strong disagreement with a professor about a lower-than-expected grade you received on a term paper. Immediately, a feeling of anger arises that automatically sets off a lightning-fast cascade of physiological processes. "This is totally unfair," you say to yourself. Your angry response arouses the autonomic nervous system (ANS), which instantly and profoundly affects your body's glands and organs.

The Autonomic Nervous System (ANS)

The ANS is that part of our physiology that regulates our internal systems, such as heart rate, breathing and digestion. The ANS actually comprises two separate systems: the "sympathetic" system, which in general speeds things up; and the "parasympathetic" system, which slows things down. Without the sympathetic part of our nervous system, we wouldn't be able to get up in the morning and go about our activities, and without the parasympathetic, we wouldn't be able to relax and go to sleep at night. Ideally, these two systems operate like two synchronized teams skillfully supporting each other with a minimum of tension by making adjustments whenever something disturbs our equilibrium.

The trouble is that stress causes these two systems to get out of sync. In the example of the grade dispute with the professor, the sympathetic side keeps getting triggered because you can't stop thinking about the "injustice" of it.

The sympathetic system also has a regulatory role in the release of stress hormones such as adrenaline and cortisol. When we experience the kinds of emotions we normally feel during a conflict, they set in motion a flood of hormones and neural signals that accelerate breathing and heart rate, tighten muscles and activate sweat glands. This rapid response occurs unconsciously and is automatic for the vast majority of us.

When it comes to something such as a disputed grade, it's difficult to think about anything other than the situation we are emotionally invested in at that moment. That's because when the two branches of our ANS get out of sync, our higher brain functioning is inhibited. When our bodies are responding to a perceived threat, or experiencing a high degree of emotional stress, we can't do the kind of clear thinking needed to successfully participate in a discussion, write a paper or adequately address an issue at home or school. Instead, our survival instincts take over.

Our Range of Responses to Stress

We have three basic responses – *fight, flight* or *freeze* – to any perceived threat hard-wired into our brain's and body's neural circuits. Fortunately, we humans have additional options besides these instinctive responses. For example, in the case of the disputed grade, instead of fighting, fleeing or freezing, we can calm down and rationally discuss our disagreement with the professor. We know from what we have read, heard or experienced that we can be rational, good-mannered and show understanding of others' points of view. These sorts of responses enable us to have positive or collaborative relationships with others, even if we don't personally like them or share their values.

When we're in conflict with others, we may revert to a reactive and defensive emotional state, thus adversely affecting our ability to cooperate and collaborate. That's because the more highly developed part of our brain – the frontal cortex – is harder to access and doesn't function very well alongside a much noisier state of emotional agitation.

The Fight or Flight Response

Whether our emotions erupt into a heated argument with the professor or are bottled up inside out of some sense of social etiquette, we nonetheless are affected by stressful situations. The ancient fight-or-flight survival response was critical when our ancestors needed to protect themselves from wild animals and marauding bands of barbarians. They had to confront the threat or get away from it as quickly as possible. Although normally we no longer face such dangers, our bodies can still react to stressful situations as if they were life threatening. Even in mildly threatening situations, this hard-wired system can still cause us to respond as if we were coming face to face with a saber-toothed tiger or Conan the Barbarian. Even the sight of a tiger, uh...er...a professor, an overly talkative roommate, or the thought of a midterm or letter about an overdue bill can ignite these ancient responses. When this happens, the signals sent through the ANS trigger our adrenal glands and within seconds our bodies respond the same as if our lives actually depended on our ability to outrun a four-legged beast.

Because fighting or fleeing are not usually options, all of the changes in our hormones, metabolism, etc., can cause us to feel as if we're about to explode. At the same time, we are burning lots of extra energy and that can leave us feeling drained or depressed. Each time we think about a problem, the complex nervous system and biochemical processes associated with emotional stress are reactivated, thus creating a vicious downward cycle.

The Freeze Response

For some people, stress can have such a powerful effect that instead of "fight or flight, they experience "freeze," a fear response that renders them incapable of acting or making decisions. At such times, they procrastinate or, worse, retreat into a state of emotional paralysis. Like a mouse whose final survival instinct with a stalking cat is to simply collapse in surrender, dissociating itself from any pain and threat, we unconsciously employ this third type of response as a final effort to deal with stressful situations. In the conflict with the professor, the freeze response attempts to numb us from any thought or feeling on the matter. This explains why some people escape stressful situations by going to a movie, sleeping two days straight, eating two jumbo hamburgers or getting drunk – anything to block out what they are feeling. This freeze response applies to communication issues, academic deadlines, paying bills, making weighty decisions or anything else we find threatening.

Sooner or later you are likely to encounter rude people, boring classes, overly stern professors, extremely high-priced books or a foot-high stack of required reading. If you habitually react to these sorts of things with frustration, anxiety or avoidance, and you don't do anything to diminish their hold on you, your ANS will stay in an over-active mode, your higher brain processes will shut down, and you will wonder why you feel overwhelmed, in mental gridlock and totally exhausted at the end of the day.

This handbook can help you learn to manage the instinctive fight, flight or freeze responses. Maintaining composure in stressful situations empowers you to respond more calmly and intelligently. You can start by learning practices to help you self-regulate your emotions, which are the primary drivers of activity in your ANS and greatly influence the neural signals flowing between your heart and brain.

The Heart-Brain Connection

Most of us have been taught that the heart is constantly responding to "commands" sent by the brain in the form of neural activity. It is not commonly known, however, that the heart actually sends more signals to the brain than the brain sends to the heart. These heart signals have a significant effect on brain function, influencing emotional processing and higher cognitive faculties such as attention, perception, memory and problem-solving.[1] In other words, not only does the heart respond to the brain, but the brain continuously responds to the heart.

Various patterns of heart activity that accompany different emotional states have distinct effects on cognitive and emotional functioning. During stressful emotions, when heart-rhythm patterns are erratic and disordered, the pattern of neural signals traveling from the heart to the brain inhibits higher cognitive functions – a process known as *cortical inhibition*.[2] This limits our ability to think clearly, remember, learn, reason and make effective decisions, which helps explain why we often may act impulsively and unwisely when we're under stress.

When you are overly anxious about money or a new relationship or how you will do on a test, your anxiety keeps your brain from functioning at its best. This is why, even when you have studied hard for an exam and know the material, you might not do well because anxiety is impeding your ability to remember what you've studied and use your problem-solving skills.

In contrast, the more ordered and stable pattern of the heart's input to the brain during positive emotional states has the opposite effect. This pattern, which promotes and enables cognitive function through the process known as *cortical facilitation*, reinforces positive feelings and emotional stability.[3] This means that learning to generate increased heart-rhythm *coherence* – an optimal state of physical, mental and emotional harmony and balance – not only benefits the entire body, but also profoundly affects how we perceive, think, feel and perform.

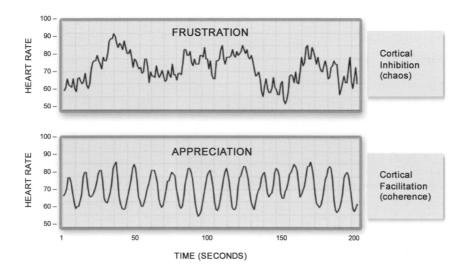

Heart-rhythm patterns during different emotional states. These graphs show examples of real-time heart rate variability patterns (heart rhythms) recorded from individuals experiencing different emotions. The incoherent heart-rhythm pattern shown in the top graph, characterized by its irregular, jagged waveform, is typical of stressful emotions such as anger, frustration and anxiety. The bottom graph shows an example of the coherent heart-rhythm pattern that typically is observed when an individual is experiencing a sustained positive emotion such as appreciation, compassion or love. The coherent pattern is characterized by its regular, sine-like waveform.[4]

The Importance of Managing Your Emotions

Emotions command our attention. If you think about your average day, you might observe how your emotions influence cognitive activity in subtle yet crucial ways.

It is hard to study when you are nervous about a recent overdue paper or you are thinking about a date the previous night with a new and exciting person in your life. Emotions also influence memory and learning. Although you probably can't recall what you had for dinner three nights ago, you can easily recall a favorite memory from your youth.

Emotions also affect judgment and decision-making. We all would like to think of ourselves as being objective, but often our emotions bias our opinions. Even when a referee mistakenly penalizes our favorite football team's archrival, we cheer at the top of our lungs, but we are incensed at the perceived injustice when a penalty is called against our team.

Although two-way communication between the cognitive and emotional systems is hard-wired into the brain, the actual number of neural connections going from emotional processing areas to cognitive centers is greater than the number going the other way. This explains the powerful influence emotions have on our thought processes. Being able to identify and manage emotions is an important skill not only for reducing stress, but also for cognition, decision-making and performance.

Questions to Ponder

1. In what ways do you experience fight, flight or freeze?
2. In what ways do your classmates or family members experience fight, flight or freeze?
3. Identify a time when you experienced cortical facilitation. In what ways were you thinking more clearly? Write these down. (*For example, was it easier to make decisions?*)
4. Think about a time when you experienced cortical inhibition. In what ways were you thinking less clearly? Write these down. (*For example, was it harder to focus during your professors' lectures?*)

Chapter 3

Performance and Stress

A manager at Microsoft told a story about an executive at another company encouraging him to apply for a senior position with his firm. He decided to test the waters and went through the job interview. Part of the process was sending in his college transcript, something he was reluctant to do because he did not meet the minimum 3.0 GPA requirement. What he did instead was go to his parents' house, dig through his old paperwork and fax over his impressive-looking report card from the third grade. He didn't get the job, of course, but the company appreciated his humor.[1]

One type of stress common to almost all students is the pressure to achieve academic success. Although not every student is focused on earning a high GPA, most want to do well in their studies in preparation for graduate school, getting a job or advancing in their present employment. Companies hiring college graduates look at a range of factors, including grades.

In its Job Outlook 2011, the National Association of Colleges and Employers (NACE) found GPA screening was on the rise.

"More than three out of four respondents said they will screen Class of 2011 job candidates by GPA – an all-time high," NACE reported. "The most popular GPA cut-off is 3.0, cited by 64 percent of those who reported their cut-off and consistent with results of surveys stretching back to 2003."[2]

The obvious conclusion from these statistics is that most college students have to apply themselves academically if they are to compete successfully in today's job market. That can put a lot of pressure on a student's shoulders.

That doesn't mean, however, a student with an average GPA can't land a quality job. Besides GPA and job-specific skills, employers look at factors such as communication, leadership, problem-solving skills, creativity and planning. Personal values such as honesty, dedication, reliability and professionalism are important to employers, who also take a hard look at students who work their way through school. Of lesser importance, some recent studies show, are students' extracurricular activities and their colleges' reputations.

A good academic record certainly always will be advantageous, but a straight-A student with weak interpersonal skills might not fare as well with an employer as one who has strong interpersonal skills and a respectable academic record. In other words, an academically successful and well-balanced student could have some advantages over one who is focused primarily on GPA.

Handling Pressure

As you may remember from the previous chapter, when you experience a challenge like a midterm, your hormonal system and the sympathetic branch of your nervous system are activated, and for a short time your performance may improve. This explains why many people believe stress motivates them. It can initially, but at a certain point, as the level of challenge increases or even remains consistent over time, your performance level becomes compromised. You find yourself working longer and harder just to keep up. You also may find yourself reacting quicker with irritation or anger to events and people. Most people don't notice when their performance begins to slip, but eventually they recognize the signs of overstress.

In the graph on the next page, you can see that initially, when we take on a challenge, our performance increases; the term *good stress* comes from this. As the challenge persists, however, and creates additional stress, performance levels out and eventually drops off dramatically. This phase is accompanied by feelings of exhaustion and, if not addressed successfully, leads to what is called the breakdown phase. Generally, this kind of breakdown is physical, mental and emotional.[3]

Signs that you may be on the downslope include loss of focus and mental clarity, increased negative attitudes and emotions, inability to relax or sleep, physical and emotional exhaustion, strained relationships and difficulty motivating yourself.

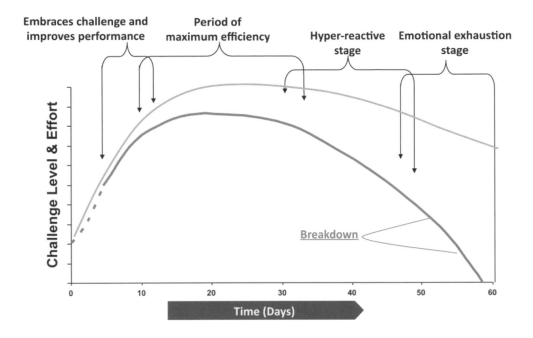

In the graph above, the upper and lower arcs show the changes in resilience levels of two people over 60 days. The lower arc represents an individual with fewer coping skills. When each is faced with a challenge, initially resilience and performance increase. As the challenge continues, resilience and performance begin declining, even more rapidly for the individual represented by the lower arc.

People experience the peak of the curve differently, depending on their emotional resilience. Those with more resilience perform at higher levels for longer periods. Those with less resilience reach their peak earlier and have less capacity for coping and adapting and greater tendency for exhaustion and illness. Even those with high resilience will succumb to exhaustion and illness if the challenge lasts long enough.

Amir's Story

Amir spent three tours of duty as a Marine, two in Iraq and one in Afghanistan. After four years of active duty, he wanted to begin his college education despite some doubts about his academic readiness. During his first semester, he struggled to get a 2.0 average. Amir was not used to the constant studying. He felt he should do better, but his brain and body were not always fully engaged. The pressure to succeed sometimes made him feel moody. Plus, he had difficulty relating to the thousands of people at the sprawling urban campus where he was studying. His sleep was interrupted by unpleasant memories and dreams from his combat history. A college counselor suggested he join a vet support group and drop one or two of his classes so he wouldn't feel so stressed.

According to research conducted by the Albert Einstein College of Medicine, "Excessive and prolonged stress can cause emotional and physical exhaustion. Students may lose interest in work they once enjoyed. They lose energy, and may feel like they cannot function anymore.[4]

Dr. Julia Moss, a psychologist at the University of Massachusetts, Amherst, described what occurs in scenarios like Amir's.

"As stress goes up a little bit, your performance does go up," Moss explained, "but at some point, if you have too many demands, your performance will start going down because it would just feel like too much. You wouldn't be able to perform at all."

She said the symptoms of stress are "low energy, lowered resistance to illness, headaches and stomachaches," and that they can lead to "emotional exhaustion." Students who reach the point of emotional exhaustion often withdraw socially. It is as if the light bulb inside gets turned off. This is especially true when a college student is coping with multiple pressures such as academic deadlines, upcoming exams, tight budgets and relationship issues.

"They start feeling isolated and emotionally depleted," Moss said.[5]

Transforming the Stress Response

Like everyone, you need tools that help relieve stress on the spot or, even better, prevent stress before it happens. Often, people respond to stressors by looking for quick cures for their discomfort – going out for a drink with buddies, watching a movie, eating something sweet or even skipping class. These can change the way you feel in the moment, but they won't change your stress habits or the inevitable wear and tear that accompany them. Learning to manage your emotions *when* you experience stress, not just after the fact, is what gives you the ability to cope with and transform stress. You will learn the first steps for neutralizing stress in the next chapter.

Everyday Emotions

We all experience a wide array of emotions, from smoldering resentment to white-hot anger, peaceful calm to exuberant joy. This range of emotions, in fact, is what distinguishes us from other animals and contributes to the richness of human experience. We would soon be exhausted if we only felt anger or joy, and we would quickly despair if the range of our emotions only consisted of depression or calmness. It is the dynamic interplay of all of our emotions that makes life so interesting – and so challenging.

It is our emotions that tell us whether we like or dislike something, are comfortable or uncomfortable, feel safe or unsafe. They motivate and move us to action. As neuroscientist Antonio Damasio has demonstrated through his research, without emotions, we wouldn't survive very long.[6]

Some of our emotional responses, however, are too impulsive, immature or chaotic. We may find ourselves in a rut of predictable behavior that does not serve us well such as being easily angered, constantly anxious, overly dramatic, too apathetic, frequently frustrated or chronically depressed. These habitual emotional responses interfere with our performance, decision-making and relationships. We need to recognize how and when these responses show up before we can begin managing them.

Our Emotional Landscape

We experience all of our emotions on what you could call an *Emotional Landscape* – where we live our lives.

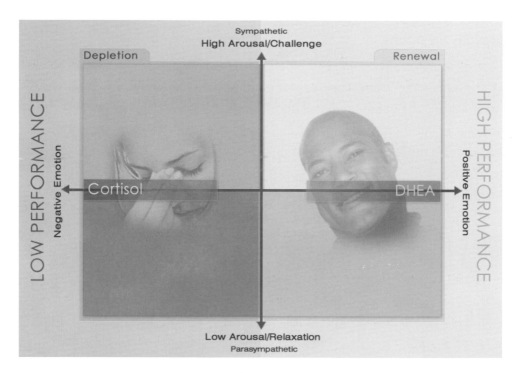

The illustration on the previous page shows that emotions can reflect either high or low arousal, high or low energy, as well as a change in the ratio of DHEA to cortisol that various emotions trigger in our bodies. (DHEA is often called the "anti-aging" or "vitality hormone." It diminishes when we experience long periods of stress. Cortisol is known as the "stress hormone" because we produce more of it when we are stressed.)

High-energy emotions, which can be either negative or positive, activate our sympathetic nervous system. Examples of negative high-energy/high-arousal emotions include anger, hostility, frustration and rage. Positive high-energy/high-arousal emotions include exhilaration, excitement, passion, joy and happiness.

Low-energy emotions reflect more parasympathetic activity and also can be experienced as either positive or negative emotions. Negative low-energy/low-arousal emotions include hopelessness, resignation, despair, depression, sadness and apathy. Positive low-energy/low-arousal emotions include compassion, forgiveness, serenity, peacefulness and care.

Some emotions can fit in both the low- and high-energy quadrants, depending on their intensity. For example, anger can be experienced as a kind of a quiet smoldering emotion or it can be expressed as shouting and verbal hostility.

Although it is completely natural and even appropriate at times to feel sad or angry, bored or frustrated, such feelings can be counterproductive when they occupy too much time and drain too much energy. When you pay attention to your emotions and actually manage them, you exercise more control over the degree of their intensity, thereby bringing more balance to your emotions and your life.

Evaluating Your Past Few Days

What does your Emotional Landscape look like? A simple way to find out is to take a sheet of paper and divide it into four quadrants matching those in the illustration on the next page. (Or, use the Emotional Landscape worksheet on page 76.)

Now, review your life over the past two or three days, and make a list of any activities, situations, conversations and events in which you were engaged. Do your best to use one or two words to describe each of your moods or emotions during these activities, and write the words in the appropriate quadrant. For example, a negative, low-arousal emotion like boredom would go in the lower left-hand quadrant, and a positive, high-arousal emotion like excitement would go in the upper right-hand quadrant.

Write down as many emotions as you can recall during this time period on your Emotional Landscape. Then step back and take a look at it.

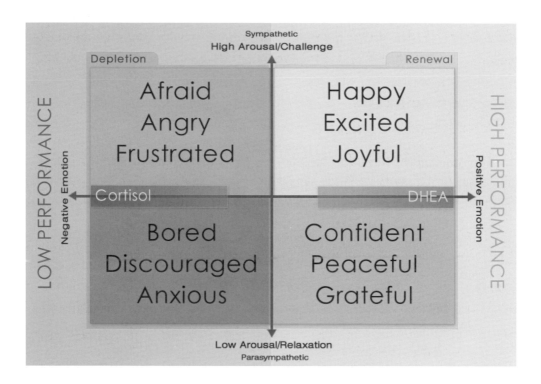

Go to www.heartmath.org/collegehandbook for more information on the Emotional Landscape.

What should emerge is a snapshot of your emotional life over the period. When you evaluate yourself, are you satisfied with the picture you see? Are there specific emotional habits that are not so healthy and need adjustment?

For example, what if a good friend called at the last minute to cancel plans for a concert and you got upset? You could let your disappointment fester and run its course until you become resentful. Many people do. Rather than carry around all that emotional drama, a more constructive approach would be to redirect your energy into several other optional activities: find someone else to go to the concert or seek out some other fun activity to counter the disappointment.

You will learn skills and strategies in the coming chapters to help you live more of your life on the side of the Emotional Landscape that renews, rather than on the one that depletes. These can benefit you during your college years and the rest of your life.

Questions to Ponder

1. How do you know when your performance is slipping?

2. If you have ever been physically and/or emotionally exhausted, how long did it take you to recover? What specifically did you do to get back to a normal and more balanced state?

3. What are two or three of the most common emotions you experience in a week? Typically, what kind of events trigger these emotional responses?

4. Are there predictable events in your schedule during which you experience emotions more on the left side of the Emotional Landscape grid? The right side?

Chapter 4

Building Coherence

We're all familiar with those clichéd sport movies in which an athlete looks up into a huge crowd and somehow spots a loved one and, from that brief moment of eye contact is inspired to perform a miraculous last-second feat to win the game. It's fun to fantasize about having such superhero-like powers to help us win a lottery and pay off our college loans, come up with a brilliant idea in class that wows the professor, or speed-read through long assignments with perfect comprehension.

Eventually, we come back to Earth, knowing we have to deal with real life. At the same time, most of us have had experiences in which everything has gone smoothly and we performed at our best. Our focus is clear, our thinking sharp and normal stressors or distractions don't interrupt our energy flow. Some researchers refer to this state as *coherence*.[1]

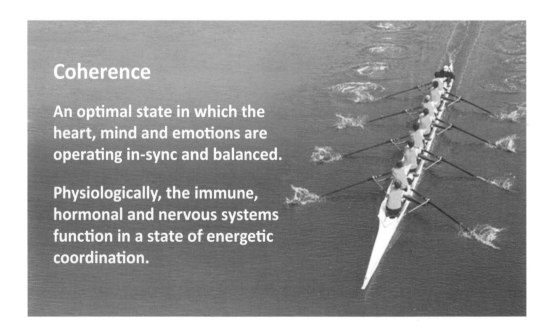

Coherence

An optimal state in which the heart, mind and emotions are operating in-sync and balanced.

Physiologically, the immune, hormonal and nervous systems function in a state of energetic coordination.

Think of coherence as an optimal state of being, learning and performance in which we are functioning at our best. We sometimes refer to this state as "flow," "peak experience" and "being in the zone." Because we often tend to be more familiar with the opposite state – incoherence – we have an idea of how difficult it is to maintain coherence. This chapter will teach you how to self-generate coherence and cultivate more resilience in your life.

Henry J. Kahn, M.D., director of student health and counseling services at the University of California, San Francisco, likens coherence to the readiness position in tennis. "Tennis players are typically not in one rigid posture," Kahn observes. "As they wait for a serve or a volley, they are poised to go in any direction, left or right, forwards or backwards. In the same way, coherence helps us be more flexible in response to whatever comes our way."

Institute of HeartMath director of research, Dr. Rollin McCraty, describes coherence in more physiological terms: "It is an optimal state in which the heart, mind and emotions operate in sync and are balanced," McCraty explained. "There is increased order and harmony in ANS activity and increased heart–brain synchronization."[2]

Resilience

There is a strong relationship between coherence and resilience. The more we achieve coherence, the more we strengthen our resilience. Resilience is the ability to adapt to, recover from or adjust to change or adversity. Qualities of resilience include flexibility, hardiness, hopefulness and persistence.

Life's difficulties and stresses don't suddenly vanish because we build up our resilience. Rather, resilience is an internal quality that gives us the resourcefulness and strength to tackle problems head-on, overcome hardships and refocus on what is important.

Nelson Mandela and Anne Frank are two remarkable examples of resilient people: Mandela, the resistance leader who survived 17 years in prison for his opposition to apartheid in South Africa, later became the nation's president and won the Nobel Peace Prize. Anne Frank, the young Jewish girl who died in a German concentration camp, wrote her famous diary while in hiding from the Nazis with her family during World War II; her story of resilience has inspired millions around the world.

Both Mandela and Frank had the inner strength to persist amid adversity and believed they could overcome any obstacles they encountered. Resilient people tend to be more optimistic and hopeful than those who are not, according to various studies, including a 2006 study of Texas A&M University students that found a direct correlation between hope and resilience.[3]

Key Moments of Stress

Rarely does a day go by when we don't experience some kind of stress that may affect our coherence and resilience. One minute we're feeling on top of the world and suddenly something happens or someone says or does something that brings us down. Suppose, for example, we go to class prepared to take an exam, only to find that the first question causes us to panic and forget everything we've learned. When this happens, we are likely to carry these feelings of disappointment, hurt or frustration for hours afterward, which can erode our coherence and resilience.

An unexpected test question, an insult or almost anything, real or imagined, can send our whole system into chaos or incoherence. Even anticipating we will not do well on a test, that a certain professor is going to be difficult, or a person who was rude and obnoxious to us today will behave the same way tomorrow is enough to upset our emotional balance.

Being aware of and then neutralizing such stressful feelings, preferably when they first happen, are key opportunities for taking action to preserve our emotional balance. That means not losing our cool while we take some time to get a clearer perspective and come up with a strategy for addressing a stressful situation.

> **"I try to take one day at a time, but sometimes several days attack me at once."**
>
> — *Jennifer Yane, comedian*

"One of the most important things I teach my students is to be aware of how stressful events affect their bodies and how to respond with more emotional intelligence," adds Dr. Ron Leslie, a psychology professor at the University of Cincinnati, Clermont.

The Quick Coherence® Technique

There are several techniques and practices in this book that show you how to transform stress, thereby increasing your coherence and building resilience. The simplest is the Quick Coherence® Technique. Quick Coherence can be easily learned and used in any situation that requires you to counter stress. People worldwide use this technique to remain resilient and effective in the face of change and challenge. Quick Coherence, which takes as little as one to two minutes, can be employed first thing in the morning to help you prepare for the day, between or during classes, before or during social events, or anytime you feel overloaded and pressed for time. One of the advantages of this technique is that you can do it without anyone knowing.

The Two Steps of the Quick Coherence Technique*

Step 1. Heart-Focused Breathing

Imagine your breath is flowing in and out of the heart area or center of your chest to help you calm down and reduce the intensity of a stress-producing reaction. Take slow, deep breaths; inhale for 5 seconds and exhale for 5 seconds.

One of the advantages of breathing slowly and deeply through the area of the heart is that it helps balance the two branches of your nervous system while interrupting your body's stress response. This can result in a more coherent heart-rhythm pattern.

Step 2. Activate a Positive Feeling

Activate a positive feeling such as appreciation or care for a special person or pet, or you could recall an enjoyable occasion or special place that made you feel good inside. Try to re-experience that feeling now.

*Modified from the original Quick Coherence Technique

Did you know?

According to Barbara Frederickson, one of the world's authorities on the importance of positive emotions, humans are genetically programmed to seek positive emotions such as love and joy.[4]

Making Quick Coherence a New Habit

The Quick Coherence Technique is very simple, but each step is important and requires focused attention. Otherwise, if you are not sincere in your practice, it can become a hollow exercise. Remember:

- *Heart-Focused Breathing* shifts your system into increased coherence because your breath's rhythm modulates your heart's rhythm.

- *Activating a Positive Feeling* helps you sustain coherence.

For Quick Coherence to become a new habit, it is best to create a regular routine in which you practice it two to three times a day for several minutes each time. It might take three to four weeks of practice for this to become a new norm. It is probably best not to begin your practice at the height of a stressful experience because your normal fight/flight/freeze response might be activated before you have a chance to neutralize it.

Professor Leslie tells his students upfront that they have to become proficient in Quick Coherence if they want it to be effective.

"Because we are a nation of shallow breathers, I guide my students in how to breathe more deeply," Leslie said. "When they become more conscious of their breathing, then I have them activate a positive emotion like appreciation. Repetition is important. If they take it seriously, there are some really positive benefits."

Recommended Practice Times

Practicing the Quick Coherence Technique two or three times per day will benefit you mentally, emotionally and physically. *Choose from the following times or select others that work for you.*

- When you first wake up

- Driving to school or walking to class

- Before class

- During stressful times in class

- During a pause or lull in meetings

- Waiting in line

- During a break

- Going from work to school or from school to home

- Quiet moments at home

- Before and during sporting activities

- Before going to sleep

Daily Applications

Once you have become comfortable practicing the two steps of the Quick Coherence Technique, you can apply it in any situation: when you first start to feel the stress of the day, when you open your email or your Facebook page, before or during a test, when communicating with a difficult person, when you feel overloaded or pressed for time, or anytime you simply want to practice increasing your coherence.

Darnell's Story

Darnell felt anxious a lot during the first semester of his sophomore year at a Missouri university. During a visit to the college counseling center, he was introduced to the Quick Coherence Technique. After practicing it for several weeks, he reported that his second semester was progressing much more smoothly.

"At first I found doing Quick Coherence a little awkward," Darnell said. "I think I was self-conscious about breathing in a new way. It took a bit of practice to feel comfortable with it. Now I use Quick Coherence in a lot of situations. If I am feeling nervous about talking to a professor, I just go through the steps until my anxiety is under control. I've used it before taking a test or writing a paper. I've even found it useful when talking to my Dad. We haven't always had the best relationship."

Using emWave® Technology to Boost Your Practice

Many college counseling, academic support and campus health and wellness centers use innovative technologies like the emWave® Desktop or emWave2®, a handheld device, to help students deal with stressful feelings. These kinds of technologies are becoming more common because they are proving themselves effective in helping students learn and reinforce emotion self-regulation techniques such as Quick Coherence.

The emWave Desktop helps train students to achieve coherence by demonstrating in real time on a computer screen how emotions and attitudes are affecting their heart-rhythm patterns. Using a pulse sensor plugged into a computer's USB port and attached to a student's earlobe, the emWave Desktop collects pulse data and then translates that information into user-friendly graphics that display levels of coherence. Through coherence techniques, game play and recorded sessions, students learn to build greater resilience and increase focus and self-control.

The emWave2 is a handheld, portable heart-rate monitor that measures subtle changes in your heart rhythms. This versatile device provides input on heart-rhythm data using colorful lights and sound to help users increase their coherence levels wherever they are. The emWave2, which is used by a wide range of athletes, health-care professionals and business people, interfaces with your computer to show graphically each session of heart-rhythm data, review previous sessions or play one of the interactive coherence-building games.

As reported in the *College Student Journal*, "Students learn to produce heart rhythms that are associated with positive emotions which reduce their stress level and improve their overall well-being."[5] Check with your college counseling center to see if the emWave Desktop, the emWave2 or other self-regulation technologies are available. They can be a fun and effective way of learning how to build up and maintain coherence.

Questions to Ponder

1. Why do some people cope better than others with life's inevitable challenges and hardships?

2. Does resilience involve innate characteristics that people inherit or is it something learned over time?

3. When have you experienced moments of coherence or performed at your best?

4. Can you name two stressors or challenges you think Quick Coherence could reduce while improving your performance?

Chapter 5

Test Anxiety, Insomnia, Digital Overload and Relationships

Your contentment and focus can be disrupted at any time by all sorts of preoccupations or pulls that cause stress. This chapter will focus on four types of stress common to college students: test anxiety, insomnia, digital overload and relationships. You will learn how to use Quick Coherence and other solutions to reduce their influence whenever you sense they are affecting your resilience.

Test Anxiety

Most students experience test anxiety at some point in their academic careers. For a few, it can be a persistent problem because every test becomes a challenge to perform well and to keep their emotions under control enough to even show up for an exam.

Test anxiety can be caused by things such as poor study habits and organizational skills and ineffective time management. Lack of preparation likely will cause increased stress; however, even students who study well in advance can experience stress. It's estimated that 25 percent of students have such high levels of test anxiety that despite their preparation for an exam, they experience symptoms of physical, cognitive and emotional distress, all of which inhibit their ability to do well. Just the act of walking into a classroom knowing a test is about to be given can trigger serious anxiety. Anxiety causes your system to get out of sync, your brain to freeze and your memory of what you have studied to go out the window. As discussed earlier, cortical inhibition is the fancy term scientists use for "your brain has stopped working."

Test anxiety can have its roots as far back as elementary or middle school. A particularly judgmental or perfectionist parent or teacher or the ridicule of fellow students over your failure to do well on an exam may still awaken feelings of anxiety whenever you take a test. Although such emotional memories can still have a strong influence on the present, it is possible to weaken their effect by using the Quick Coherence Technique whenever you have an exam coming up.

Simple Tips for Improving Your Test-Taking Performance

There is no substitute for studying and careful preparation, but some of the following common-sense suggestions have helped many college students get into an optimal state of readiness for test-taking:

- Know the expectations and test-taking conditions beforehand. (What specific areas does the test cover and what instructions or guidelines have been given?)

- Plan and commit to a study schedule in advance, including the option of studying with other motivated students in small group review and discussion sessions.

- Practice good health habits, including exercise, healthy eating and getting adequate sleep that lasts 7-8 hours (especially the night before an exam). A healthy breakfast on test day improves thinking, concentration, mood and memory, while skipping breakfast reduces your mental, emotional and physical capacity.[1,2]

- Review your notes as close to exam time as possible.

- Practice the Quick Coherence Technique several times daily to keep your physiology in sync and your emotions in balance in the days leading up to the exam, especially right before and during the exam.

- Keep a healthy perspective. Although doing well on a test or paper is a worthy goal, there are many things in life that are more important. Remember, there is life after college!

Insomnia

College students are among the most sleep-deprived groups in our society. What causes sleeplessness? Among other things, the hormonal system imbalances that come from information overload, stimulation fatigue, overcommitment, and, of course, emotional stress. Although most students occasionally sacrifice some sleep to prepare for a major exam or complete a paper, if you experience sleeplessness for longer than a few days, more than likely you are suffering from stress overload. Adding caffeine and hours of social media only adds to sleeplessness.

A recent study found that chronic insomnia is associated with elevated levels of the stress hormone cortisol. It also suggested that insomniacs are at increased risk for chronic anxiety and depression. The researchers concluded that one way to decrease insomnia is to decrease the amount of emotional arousal during the day, especially in the hours before bedtime.[3] Again, practicing Quick Coherence can help calm your mind and emotions so you are better prepared for sleep at the end of the day.

The amount of sleep you get can affect learning. Through what is known as *memory consolidation*, sleep helps you process what you learned during the day. During sleep, the area of your brain where memory is stored becomes very active and moves what you have experienced and learned from short-term to long-term memory.[4] Sleep also has some important health benefits, enabling the body to rejuvenate and repair itself, strengthen the immune system, revive brain cells, and reduce fatigue and stress. Basically, we can't function with any degree of normalcy without sleep.

Below are some sleep experiences typical of college students:

- "If I could sleep regularly, I would probably be happier. Last night I went to sleep at 7 and then woke up an hour later, stayed up until 3 or 4 in the morning to write a paper and then went to sleep for an hour or two before waking up to finish it and go to class. Needless to say, I felt miserable all day."

- "I have problems with sleep because when you are trying to balance a job and college with a family, it doesn't always work with your college schedule. Having to get up in the middle of the night with a sick child the night before a big test can ruin your whole day – and your GPA."

- "If I get less than seven hours of sleep, I just don't function well at all. I find I work better, am more productive and get better grades when I get enough sleep. Also, I'm much nicer to be around!"

According to a recent report, during the last 50 years, the average night's sleep for adult Americans has shrunk from eight hours a night to six and a half.[5] No wonder our society is so exhausted and stressed much of the time.

Sometimes students have an air of invincibility when it comes to sleep. They feel they can burn the midnight oil and not experience any negative consequences. A recent article in *The New York Times* suggests otherwise: "A good night's sleep is much more than a luxury. Its benefits include improvements in concentration, short-term memory, productivity, mood, sensitivity to pain, and immune function."[6]

10 Tips for Falling and Staying Asleep
From the Mayo Clinic[7]

1. **Go to bed and get up at about the same time every day, even on the weekends.** Sticking to a schedule helps reinforce your body's sleep-wake cycle and can help you fall asleep more easily at night.

2. **Don't eat or drink large amounts before bedtime.** Eat a light dinner at least two hours before sleeping. If you're prone to heartburn, avoid spicy or fatty foods, which can make your heartburn flare and prevent a restful sleep. Also, limit how much you drink before bed. Too much liquid can cause you to wake up repeatedly during the night for trips to the toilet.

3. **Avoid nicotine, caffeine and alcohol in the evening.** These are stimulants that can keep you awake. Smokers often experience withdrawal symptoms at night, and smoking in bed is dangerous. Avoid caffeine for eight hours before your planned bedtime. Your body doesn't store caffeine, but it takes many hours to eliminate the stimulant and its effects. And although often believed to be a sedative, alcohol actually disrupts sleep.

4. **Exercise regularly.** Regular physical activity, especially aerobic exercise, can help you fall asleep faster and make your sleep more restful. However, for some people, exercising right before bed may make getting to sleep more difficult.

5. **Make your bedroom cool, dark, quiet and comfortable.** Create a room that's ideal for sleeping. Adjust the lighting, temperature, humidity and noise level to your preferences. Use blackout curtains, eye covers, earplugs, extra blankets, a fan or white-noise generator, a humidifier or other devices to create an environment that suits your needs.

6. **Sleep primarily at night.** Daytime naps may steal hours from nighttime slumber. Limit daytime sleep to about a half-hour and make it during midafternoon. If you work nights, keep your window coverings closed so that sunlight, which adjusts the body's internal clock, doesn't interrupt your sleep. If you have a day job and sleep at night, but still have trouble waking up, leave the window coverings open and let the sunlight help awaken you.

7. **Choose a comfortable mattress and pillow.** Features of a good bed are subjective and differ for each person. But make sure you have a bed that's comfortable. If you share your bed, make sure there's enough room for two. Children and pets are often disruptive, so you may need to set limits on how often they sleep in bed with you.

8. **Start a relaxing bedtime routine.** Do the same things each night to tell your body it's time to wind down. This may include taking a warm bath or shower, reading a book, or listening to soothing music. Relaxing activities done with lowered lights can help ease the transition between wakefulness and sleepiness.

9. **Go to bed when you're tired and turn out the lights.** If you don't fall asleep within 15 to 20 minutes, get up and do something else. Go back to bed when you're tired. Don't agonize over falling asleep. The stress will only prevent sleep.

10. **Use sleeping pills only as a last resort.** Check with your doctor before taking any sleep medications. He or she can make sure the pills won't interact with your other medications or with an existing medical condition. Your doctor can also help you determine the best dosage. If you do take a sleep medication, reduce the dosage gradually when you want to quit, and never mix alcohol and sleeping pills. If you feel sleepy or dizzy during the day, talk to your doctor about changing the dosage or discontinuing the pills.

Digital Overload

We live in a world of ever-expanding and increasingly sophisticated technology. Today's students can communicate instantly with people all around the globe, access vast libraries and information storehouses and store all of their communications in a device the size of a small book. In addition, they can watch TV and movies on their own electronic screens, check the weather or showtimes, watch videos on YouTube, and perform a thousand tasks that their parents could only have dreamed of doing when they were young. In other words, it is hard to imagine today's college students without all of their electronic gadgets and technology.

Despite the advantages of today's technologies, they have limitations and can interfere with schoolwork. The problem arises when you are bombarded daily with a seemingly never-ending stream of phone calls, emails, Facebook messages, text messages and tweets. You run the risk of becoming part of what is called the "culture of interruption," which makes it hard to concentrate, stay focused or think clearly and creatively. The culture of interruption is characterized by frequent interruptions and trying to do too many tasks at the same time, which can lead to scattered thinking and high levels of stress. The challenge is finding a balance between being plugged in and having more time and presence in the other areas of your life.

A popular myth on American campuses is that students can multitask without sacrificing quality or productivity. Recent studies have shown the opposite is true. Professor Clifford Nass, a specialist on chronic multitasking at Stanford University, observed, "One of the things that seems to be true is [that] people who multitask very, very frequently believe they are excellent at it, and they're actually, as far as we can tell, the worst at it of any people." He added that even when such students aren't multitasking, they show evidence of cognitive impairment.[8] This is confirmed by UCLA professor of psychology, Russell Poldrack, who said, "Multitasking adversely affects how you learn. Even if you learn while multitasking, that learning is less flexible and more specialized, so you cannot retrieve the information as easily. ... Tasks that require more attention, such as learning calculus or reading Shakespeare, will be particularly adversely affected by multitasking."[9]

Consider the effect on your brain, body, and emotions when you find yourself in the middle of composing a tweet and your computer shows an incoming message from a Facebook friend, your iPhone rings, and someone knocks at your door – all while you are trying to watch the closing minutes of the NBA finals or the last episode of *American Idol* on TV.

On one level, all of this electronic stimulation can be exciting, causing an adrenaline rush and possibly giving the illusion that you can handle all of these tasks like a circus juggler keeping five balls, four plates, and three knives in the air at the same time. If you are too fixated on your electronic gadgets, however, and are constantly juggling a steady stream of emails, phone calls, text messages and tweets, you could be experiencing "digital overload."

Common Student Experiences

"I use Facebook constantly. It's a really good procrastination tool and way to stay in touch with everyone. I use it all the time. It's the first thing I check when I turn my computer on."

"I can't live without my iPhone. I use it to tell time, check the weather, search for a restaurant, check the score of a game, do email, play games, talk to friends, text, and do all kinds of neat things with the hundred or so apps I have on it. I even set it on my nightstand when I go to sleep. And I use its alarm to wake me up in the morning. I feel like composing a song: 'Me and My iPhone.'"

"I check Facebook 3-4 times a day *(maybe thousands but I'm not admitting to that here).*"

Multitasking Versus Continuous Partial Attention

Some of the most insightful perceptions on the topic of digital connectivity are offered by former Microsoft executive, Linda Stone. She acknowledges the benefits of multitasking but within certain boundaries: "When we multitask, we are motivated by a desire to be more productive and more efficient. We often do things that are automatic, that require very little cognitive processing – we file and copy papers, talk on the phone, eat lunch – (and) we get as many things done at one time as we possibly can in order to make more time for ourselves and be more efficient and more productive."[10]

Stone contrasts this form of multitasking with what she calls "continuous partial attention," which is the epitome of digital overload. Instead of being motivated by the desire to accomplish many tasks at the same time, continuous partial attention "is motivated by a desire to … connect and be connected. We want to effectively scan for the best opportunities, activities and contacts, in any given moment. … We pay continuous partial attention in an effort NOT TO MISS ANYTHING. It is an always-on, anywhere, anytime, anyplace behavior that involves an artificial sense of constant crisis. We are always in high alert when we pay continuous partial attention."[11]

To find balance in the use of personal technology, Stone recommends asking yourself: "How do I feel? What would feel better? Your body is wiser than your mind in these matters." It is helpful during such times to step back and evaluate where you are on your Emotional Landscape. When you are plugged in, which quadrant are you in emotionally?

Stone observes that people tend to hold their breath or breathe shallowly when they are connected to their computers, smart phones and other devices. She terms this state "email apnea – a temporary absence or suspension of breathing, or shallow breathing, while doing email."[12] The breathing portion of the Quick Coherence Technique can be helpful in countering shallow breathing.

Tips for Handling Digital Overload and Continuous Partial Attention

- Unplug. Take a digital break. Turn off your digital devices for three hours or longer so your brain, body and emotions can be refreshed and you can re-establish balance.

- Pay attention to your mind, body and emotions when you are plugged in. Where are you on the Emotional Landscape?

- Whenever you become anxious about not being plugged in or even when you are plugged in, practice Quick Coherence. It can help you refocus and experience more coherence when you are engaged with electronic devices.

- Practice leaving your smartphone at home on occasion. Go outside, change environments, enjoy nature and have some live interactions with people.

- Get some exercise and physical movement. Physical exercise or movement helps get you out of your overactive brain and adds a dose of fun and positive energy.

- If you feel you are becoming addicted to electronic media, consider reading William Powers' *Hamlet's Blackberry: A Practical Philosophy for Building a Good Life in the Digital Age,* a timely book about our overdependence on electronic media. Powers observed that he and his wife and son had become so absorbed in using their computers that they missed important things all around them, especially interactions with one another. They decided to turn off their computer and other devices every weekend. Since then, he said, "We really enter this other zone, and it's wonderful. ... It's just about that simple word, 'balance.' "[13]

Most college students would likely find that being disconnected for as long as Powers' family would be a daunting challenge, but all of us can benefit from cutting down on electronic overdependence. All of us can be more aware of the warning signs of digital overload.

Relationships

One of the most interesting and potentially fulfilling experiences in college, whether you are a first-year freshman, returning veteran, or an older student returning to college, are the relationships you establish. Through interactions with fellow students, faculty and others you have the opportunity to enrich your life in many ways.

Students at a California university shared comments about their college relationships:

"I've met some people I greatly admire and others I wouldn't care to spend five minutes with."

"The personalities of my professors can be described as brilliant, arrogant, weird, funny, caring and deathly boring."

"Partying with someone is not the same as being a good friend."

"I've learned to be more discriminating in choosing my friends, based upon some major disappointments."

"I am surrounded by some really smart people who say and do interesting things."

"I have found that it is easy to get hurt if you aren't careful."

"I have difficulty relating to other students. Most of them seem to be in cliques, or they are too loud, too rude or too weird."

"If I can tolerate some of these juvenile idiots, I can tolerate almost anyone."

"I've made friends with people here that I expect to be friends with for the rest of my life."

Reflecting on Your College Relationships

The kinds of relationships one develops in college include acquaintances, casual and deep friendships, student-professor relationships, romantic relationships, teammates, club mates, etc. Because most college students already are overcommitted with time demands, it is wise to step back and ask yourself what kind of relationships will make college life the most satisfying and productive. What are your priorities? What is the right balance between academics, work and social life?

Because relationships often involve choices, competing needs, and personality differences, all of which can add pleasure or stress to your life, it is helpful to use some of what you have learned in this handbook to clarify what is important in your relationships.

For example, you can use the Quick Coherence Technique to prepare for a challenging encounter with someone or when you simply need to listen to another person. You also can use Quick Coherence to help you decide how to improve or end a relationship.

1. ***Heart-Focused Breathing*** helps you to stay physically and emotionally balanced as you attempt to keep a healthy perspective on relationships.

2. ***Heart Feeling*** helps you find a positive place from which you can listen with more understanding and speak honestly about your own feelings.

After you go through these two steps, ask yourself, what are the most important factors or actions to consider in maintaining healthy relationships.

If you have questions or concerns about some of your most important or closest relationships, do an Asset/Deficit Balance Sheet (Chapter 6) to get clarity. After evaluating which aspects of the relationship are supportive and which are not, do the Freeze Frame® Technique (page 54) and then draw a conclusion based on that information. Ask yourself, "Does this relationship make me happy or unhappy? Is it helping me or getting in the way of my goals?" As you review your conclusions, examine which quadrants on the Emotional Landscape are most active when you are with specific people. Taking some quiet, reflective time away from other people and distractions will allow you to evaluate whether the people with whom you are involved are meeting your relationship needs.

Relationships can be one of the best or most difficult parts of your college experience, depending on your circumstances. Some will become solid friendships strengthened by genuine support, mutual interest and care while others will be ephemeral, shallow and full of conflict and disappointment. It is particularly important in intimate relationships for you to know beforehand what your own needs, wishes and expectations are and how to set limits on what others may want or ask of you. In other words, be clear about what you choose to do freely and what your response would be to someone who is self-centered or abusive.

Obviously, there is no one-size-fits-all formula for creating and maintaining stable, mutually rewarding relationships. Such relationships often are complex because they are influenced by each individual's values, history, circumstances, needs, motives and agendas. Knowing the difference between healthy and unhealthy relationships enables you to make more intelligent choices.

Intimate Relationships

There are plenty of opportunities to meet people between classes, at organized events, parties and just hanging around campus. Inevitably, with this much social interaction, intimate relationships are bound to develop. Some last days or weeks while others endure longer – a few for a lifetime. The quality of any relationship depends on the degree of attraction and the seriousness of the bond between the partners. Is the relationship based on mutual affection and respect as well as need? Is it, by mutual agreement, a short-term relationship with mutual benefits, but no long-term obligations? Or is it an experimental relationship in which both participants are merely exploring the possibilities without any ground rules or clear communication?

The most important thing at the start of a relationship is having a clear understanding of your expectations and boundaries. If the relationship is rewarding to both people, it could lead to a more enduring partnership characterized by mutual understanding, respect, care, openness and fun. If the relationship is one-sided, however, with one person's emotional needs and expectations dominating at the other's expense, the relationship is likely to be characterized by hurt, distrust, jealousy, misunderstanding and continuing conflict, all of which will threaten the relationship and increase stress.

Questions to Ponder:

1. In what academic areas do you experience cortical inhibition? What triggers the experience and what are the symptoms?

2. Do you ever experience insomnia? If so, can you identify its causes?

3. Have you experienced the "culture of interruption"? Can you identify where it places you on the Emotional Landscape?

4. Do you experience digital overload? If so, how does it affect you?

5. Do you feel comfortable with your personal balance in relation to your studies, work, play and relationships?

Chapter 6

Time Management and Decision-Making

Because the average college student spends relatively little time in class, many students initially are under the illusion that they have an abundance of free time and flexibility in how to spend it. Once they realize how much time academic work really takes, however, along with working, commuting, socializing, social networking, engaging in extracurricular activities and taking care of basic needs, the reality of how much time they really have soon becomes apparent. That is why learning how to manage time wisely is one of the most important skills for success in college.

Perhaps no other part of our lives causes us to feel more anxious and overwhelmed than what could be called the tyranny of time – the sense that time is always flying by and there is never enough of it. Without proper time management, you can be vulnerable to high stress, become confused over priorities and perform below your potential.

As students take care to allot time for their studies, they also must guard against focusing on them or any other particular area of their lives excessively, explained Allison Reisbig, an assistant professor in the Child, Youth, and Family Studies department at the University of Nebraska, Lincoln.

"When students invest too much of their available time and energy in one area, Reisbig said, "they will experience stress from not attending to the other areas. It's important for students to diversify their commitments so that they include all areas important to them."

Although every student's situation is different, everyone is faced with decisions about how best to use their time. Choices about how you spend your time are based on your values and your priorities. Because college is a time of uncertainty and self-discovery, your ability to manage time is probably still evolving, unless you are a more experienced student.

You can be sure many unexpected distractions will come up, and they likely will put your time-management skills to the test. For instance, you may not always get all the classes you want or need. Illness or family emergencies could cause you to miss school, and you could be involved in relationships, which can sometimes be unpredictable and time-consuming. If you're like most students, you probably will change your major at least once, and along the way you will make mistakes and miscalculations that may motivate you to re-examine your priorities.

Over time, if you are diligent, you will learn what your optimal times for mental concentration and study are and schedule study blocks during these times for your most difficult classes.

Although most students don't spend excessive time on their academic work, a few do. If you are one of these, you may have to make a concerted effort to schedule time for relaxation. Conversely, if your rest and play time are excessive, you may have to discipline yourself to cut back on these. Poor time management can cause stressful feelings, which often are enough to motivate students to better manage their lives.

Five Important Skills for Time Management[1]

1. **Plan well**.
   Establish a set schedule that will help you stay organized and focused on what needs to be done. If, for example, you have a midterm, paper, lab report, research project or other task due in one month, don't procrastinate. Manage your time and workload so you have a steady flow going instead of trying to do everything in a last-minute surge.

2. **Say "no."**
   Learning to say "no" is challenging for most people because it's hard to resist the temptation to go to all of the places where we are invited and do all of the enjoyable things there are to do.

   In contrast, saying "yes" to everything can lead to impossible demands on your time. Of course, you will want to schedule some "yes" time – for family, friends, recreation, etc. – to maintain balance and a sense of well-being, but not at the expense of your academic work. The important thing to remember is that you have exactly the same number of hours in your day as anyone else, and that includes the president of the United States – the leader of the free world!

3. Choose the right study environment.

With so many demands on your time and attention, including a steady bombardment of digital information and communication, finding a quiet place to study is essential for doing your best school-work. Find someplace where you can get the most out of your study time – away from friends and family, loud music or other potential distractions. Some students find it hard to unplug from social media, but this is the kind of self-discipline you will need to concentrate on your work and use the time you have most efficiently.

4. Prioritize and reprioritize.

The unexpected happens to all of us. We get sick, our computers crash, friends or family members' crises pull us in, we change our majors, and we fall in love. These are the kinds of things that are bound to happen. The best time managers are those who have the ability to reprioritize when things come up and circumstances change.

When the unexpected does occur, remember what your primary goals and values are, and draw on the support of friends, family, academic counselors and others. These are things that can help you use your time most efficiently.

5. Keep yourself fit to learn.

Being ready to learn requires following some pretty basic, but critical rules. Allow your brain and body to rejuvenate by getting plenty of sleep so you can meet your demanding college schedule. Eat healthy meals, especially breakfast, so you will have the fuel you need to stay focused, think critically, have good recall and be creative.

Equally important in the learning process is managing your stress, which will help improve your mental, emotional and physical health and in turn the quality of choices you make in your diet, sleep habits, time management, schoolwork and social life. The internal stress we build up by such things as worrying or becoming frustrated over things out of our control can be reduced by consciously devoting a little time each day to managing stressful feelings. Daily stress maintenance actually will end up saving you time in the long run.

Decision-making

One of the biggest challenges facing college students is making good decisions. Over the course of your college years, you will make many decisions that will have both immediate and future consequences.

Having lots of options and a busy schedule can make decision-making complex and difficult, especially when we experience what is known as *information fatigue.* This term, which was recently added to the Oxford English Dictionary, is defined as "apathy, indifference or mental exhaustion arising from exposure to too much information; stress induced by the attempt to assimilate excessive amounts of information from the media, the Internet, or at work."[2]

Too much information creates mental and emotional overload, causing the brain to stretch beyond its normal capacity. When our frustration and anxiety soar, our body's stress response makes it hard to focus, prioritize and make good decisions. Under pressure, we make impulsive decisions and unwise choices. Basically, we lose our perspective on what is important.

Steve Jobs of Apple Computers, speaking at a college commencement, talked about the importance of being guided by your heart and intuition.

"Your time is limited, so don't waste it living someone else's life. Don't be trapped by dogma, which is living with the results of other people's thinking. Don't let the noise of others' opinions drown out your own inner voice. And, most important, have the courage to follow your heart and intuition. They somehow already know what you truly want to become. Everything else is secondary."[3]

Freeze Frame When Making Decisions and Solving Problems

As you have learned in this handbook, stress impedes good decision-making and problem-solving. Freeze Frame is an effective technique in which you take a step back from a stress response such as feeling frustrated or overwhelmed to gather more clarity about a decision or issue. Freeze Frame, which is based on years of scientific research on emotional physiology and optimal function, is widely used by corporate executives, doctors, nurses, athletes, firefighters, police officers, soldiers and students. It's designed to help you take a time-out and get a smarter perspective, especially when making important decisions or when you feel challenged or stressed.

A basketball coach calls a time-out when the team isn't doing well, giving players a chance to step back, regroup, make adjustments in their strategy and perhaps change the momentum of the game. Similarly, Freeze Frame is designed to let you pause, step back and get a wider and more balanced view of any situation. Then you can ask yourself, "What is the best way to handle this situation?"

Freeze Frame consists of five simple steps you can take to stop the chaos in your brain and nervous system so you can make wiser decisions. With practice, you will see problems more clearly and have a broader range of possible responses. Freeze Frame can work during a stressful situation or when you are feeling overwhelmed about all the things you have to do. Of course, that doesn't mean issues will suddenly go away, but Freeze Frame will help you respond to them more intelligently and that will improve your chances for better outcomes.

Freeze Frame® Technique

1. Identify

Identify the problem (*decision*) or issue and any stressful feelings or reactions related to it.

2. Heart-Focused Breathing

Imagine your breath is flowing in and out of your heart area to help you calm down and reduce the intensity of a stress-producing reaction. Take slow, deep breaths; inhale for 5 seconds and exhale for 5 seconds. (*Continue until you have reduced the emotional charge around the issue.*)

3. Activate

Make a sincere effort to *activate* a positive feeling. (*This can be a genuine feeling of appreciation or care for someone, some place, or something in your life. It's important to truly be in touch with the feeling, not just think about it.*)

4. Ask

From a more objective place, *ask* yourself what would be an efficient, effective attitude, action or solution. (*Try to select a less stressful perspective, even if you can't see it clearly at first.*)

5. Observe

Quietly *observe* any thoughts, feelings or perceptions that could add clarity to the situation and commit to acting on them. (*If no insights come up, that's OK. Repeat the process later or the next day.*)

How It Works

The Freeze Frame Technique is effective because it involves aligning your mind, heart and body, which improves mental functioning and helps connect you with your intuitive capacities when you are making decisions. You may have found in the past that the more you thought about a problem and the harder you concentrated on finding an answer, the more difficult and confusing it was to see a clear answer. By shifting into a more coherent state, you will find it is easier to see the full dimensions of a problem and the possible options for solving it.

As with anything, becoming proficient at this new skill takes practice. Don't expect instant illumination when applying Freeze Frame, but if you are genuinely seeking greater clarity on an issue or decision, this technique can help you. The following exercise will give you a chance to try it out.

Freeze Frame Exercise Instructions

Part 1:
To begin, answer the first two sections on the following page as preparation for doing the Freeze Frame Exercise.

Part 2:
Review the example on page 57 as a guide.

Part 3:
Pick one of your stressors or issues that you listed in Part 1 and transfer that information to the blank Freeze Frame worksheet on page 58. Write a sentence or two about your reaction to this issue. Then try out the 5-step technique yourself, filling in the Effective Action or Attitude section at the bottom of the worksheet page to complete the exercise.

Freeze Frame® Exercise: Preparation for Using a Worksheet

Part 1: In the space below, identify two or three problems or issues that you are facing or that are causing you stressful feelings right now. They could be related to your schoolwork, job, finances, family, friends or an important personal decision you need to make.

_____

_____

_____

Now, make a short list of things you appreciate or care about – something that gives you an uplifting feeling. It could be someone you care about, some special music, a special place or a fond memory.

_____

_____

_____

Part 2: Review the Freeze Frame Exercise example on the next page as a guide.

Part 3: Pick one decision or issue from the stressors you listed in Part 1 to try out the Freeze Frame Technique. Write the issue on the Freeze Frame Worksheet on page 58. Don't pick your biggest decision or problem for your first try. Now, write a sentence or two on what your thoughts have been on this issue and what you have been feeling. Choose one thing from your appreciation list to use in Step 3 of the Freeze Frame Technique.

Practice steps 2-5 of Freeze Frame and then complete the rest of the worksheet.

Freeze Frame® Exercise

Step 1: Identify

Identify the problem or issue and any stressful feelings or reactions related to it.

Step 2: Heart-Focused Breathing

Imagine your breath is flowing in and out of your heart area to help you calm down and reduce the intensity of a stress-producing reaction. Take slow, casual deep breaths.

Step 3: Activate

Make a sincere effort to activate a positive feeling.

Step 4: Ask

From a more objective place, ask yourself what would be an efficient, effective attitude, action or solution.

Step 5: Observe

Quietly observe any thoughts, feelings or perceptions that could add clarity to the situation and commit to acting on them.

If no insights come up, that's OK. Repeat the process later or the next day.

Decision/Issue:

High cost of transportation to college

Reaction:

Feeling anxious and upset about high cost of driving my car to and from campus

Effective Action or Attitude

Find someone to ride-share with four times a week. Check out public transportation.

Often, solutions are inspired through communicating with or getting input from others.

This technique is adapted from the original version of Freeze Frame for this book.

Freeze Frame® Exercise

Step 1: Identify

Identify the problem or issue and any stressful feelings or reactions related to it.

Step 2: Heart-Focused Breathing

Imagine your breath is flowing in and out of your heart area to help you calm down and reduce the intensity of a stress-producing reaction. Take slow, casual deep breaths.

Step 3: Activate

Make a sincere effort to activate a positive feeling.

Step 4: Ask

From a more objective place, ask yourself what would be an efficient, effective attitude, action or solution.

Step 5: Observe

Quietly observe any thoughts, feelings or perceptions that could add clarity to the situation and commit to acting on them.

If no insights come up, that's OK. Repeat the process later or the next day.

Decision/Issue:

_____

Reaction:

_____

_____

_____

Effective Action or Attitude

_____

_____

_____

_____

Often, solutions are inspired through communicating with or getting input from others.

This technique is adapted from the original version of Freeze Frame for this book.

Freeze Frame® Quick Steps

In the beginning, most students will use a Freeze Frame Worksheet to write down their thought processes. With practice, the steps can be simplified into something you can do internally anywhere or anytime.

- **Identify**

- **Heart-Focused Breathing**

- **Activate**

- **Ask/Observe**

Sarah's Story

During the second semester of her sophomore year at a university in Oregon, Sarah heard the news about a proposed hike in tuition for the following school year. Already working 20 hours a week as a waitress and taking 12 units, Sarah was worried about her ability to pay the fee increase and even considered dropping out of school for a semester to work full time. Using a Freeze Frame Worksheet, Sarah first identified the stress reaction she was experiencing (anxiety). Next, she did the breathing exercise, adding something for which she felt genuine appreciation (her mother, who was working to pay part of her housing expense). Finally, she asked for clarity on what were her best options. She came up with several options that could help her pay the increased fee and stay in school. One was to ask her manager for a slight increase in pay; another was to get a job delivering mail over the Christmas holidays. These options made her feel more hopeful about her future.

The Asset/Deficit Balance Sheet

Another useful tool to help you make more intelligent decisions is the *Asset/Deficit Balance Sheet*. This exercise has two parts.

Part 1: Write down a decision or problem that you wish to address. Frame the decision in the form of a yes or no question. List the assets or positives in one column and the deficits or negatives in the second column. Some users give points of importance for each entry, ranging from a low of one point to a high of three points. That way, an important entry is given more weight than a less important one.

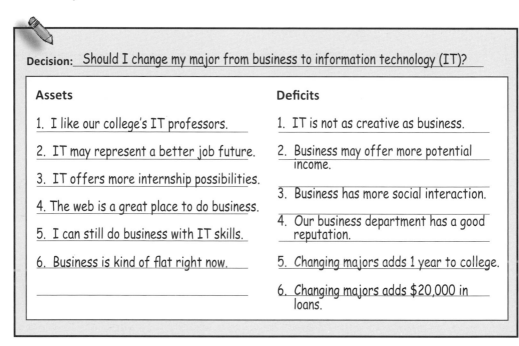

Decision: Should I change my major from business to information technology (IT)?

Assets	Deficits
1. I like our college's IT professors.	1. IT is not as creative as business.
2. IT may represent a better job future.	2. Business may offer more potential income.
3. IT offers more internship possibilities.	3. Business has more social interaction.
4. The web is a great place to do business.	4. Our business department has a good reputation.
5. I can still do business with IT skills.	5. Changing majors adds 1 year to college.
6. Business is kind of flat right now.	6. Changing majors adds $20,000 in loans.

Part 2: Once both lists are complete, use the Freeze Frame Technique to access your optimal mental, emotional and physiological state. Practicing Freeze Frame for 1-2 minutes can help neutralize any bias towards a particular outcome. Then ask yourself what is the most intelligent conclusion you can draw based on the overall information from both columns. *Do the assets outweigh the*

deficits, or vice versa? What are your intuitive feelings about the issue? Write down your conclusion. Making a decision with both quantitative and qualitative input provides the best perspective for an intelligent decision.

Steps of the Freeze Frame® Technique

- **Identify**
- **Heart-Focused Breathing**
- **Activate**
- **Ask/Observe:** (Should I change my major from business to information technology?)

Conclusion *(from example on Page 60)*:

I am leaning toward remaining a business major because it interests me more than IT, but I can take more IT classes to expand my skills. Also, I don't want to take on more debt. I will ask a career counselor for advice and I will talk with friends and family.

Asset/Deficit Tool Instructions:

Part 1: 1. Write down a decision or problem that you wish to address. Frame the decision in the form of a yes or no question.

2. Write down as many assets (positives) as you can.

3. Write down as many deficits (negatives) as you can.

4. As an option, assign one to three points to each entry based on its level of importance. Once you have assigned points, add up both the assets and deficits and subtract the difference to determine which has the highest point total.

Part 2: 1. After practicing the Freeze Frame Technique for 1-2 minutes, ask yourself the question once again.

2. Review the entries in both the Asset/Deficit columns and write down a conclusion that describes the best choice for you.

Asset/Deficit Balance Worksheet

Part 1: Write down a decision or problem that you wish to address. Frame the decision in the form of a yes or no question. List the assets or positives in one column and the deficits or negatives in the second column.

Decision:_____

Assets	Deficits

Part 2: Once both lists are complete, practice Freeze Frame for 1-2 minutes to help neutralize any bias towards a particular outcome. Then ask yourself what is the most intelligent conclusion you can draw based on the overall information from both columns.

Steps of the Freeze Frame® Technique
- Identify
- Heart-Focused Breathing
- Activate
- Ask/Observe

Conclusion:_____

Questions to Ponder:

1. What are your biggest challenges with time management?

2. Do you procrastinate? If so, how?

3. What attitudes or actions do you think contribute to students' procrastination?

4. What do you observe inside yourself mentally, emotionally and physically when you make difficult decisions?

5. What type of decisions are hard for you? What type are easy?

Chapter 7

Cool Your Heels: Flow and Inner Ease

One of the most rewarding times for college students is when they first sense that their gifts, talents and abilities are beginning to blossom. This realization is generally accompanied by increased self-confidence and a keener sense of direction and purpose. Many things become clearer. During such times, students tap into a state that heightens their focus and increases their creativity and productivity. This is sometimes referred to as "flow," a concept developed by the learning theorist, Mihaly Csikszentmihaly (me-high chick-sent-me-high-ee).

Csikszentmihalyi described flow as "the state in which people are so involved in an activity that nothing else seems to matter; the experience itself is so enjoyable that people will do it even at great cost, for the sheer sake of doing it. ... In flow, the emotions are not just contained and channeled, but positive, energized and aligned."[1] This is not some mysterious experience, but rather a state many of us have been in, often unaware we are in it or that we created it. People talk about being "in the zone," "in sync" or "in the groove" when performing at their best. Athletes, musicians, writers and others experience this, often becoming so focused or inspired that they lose track of time. The dictionary defines flow as *moving like a stream or river.*

You probably have noticed that some people often appear to be in a state of flow. Even if what they are doing is challenging, it doesn't seem to overwhelm them. One of the areas in which this is most visible is in sports. John Wooden, the legendary UCLA basketball coach, designed what he called the "Pyramid of Success," 25 foundational behaviors and qualities he believed defined success. Wooden's pyramid, which helped him build what many still consider to be the most successful college sports program in American history, identifies behaviors and qualities he considered important not only in sports but for life itself. Wooden described "poise," which he placed near the top of the pyramid, like this: "Just being yourself. Being at ease in any situation. Never fighting yourself."

Being at ease in most situations sounds challenging, but learning how to intentionally build greater poise and flow throughout the day can make your life a whole lot easier to manage. Notice as well that Wooden paired "poise" with "confidence." The two are mutually reinforcing: the more poise you have, the greater your confidence, and the more confidence you have, the greater your poise.

John Wooden's definition of success: "Success is peace of mind, which is a direct result of self-satisfaction in knowing you made the effort to do your best to become the best that you are capable of becoming."

The Inner-Ease™ Technique

The Inner-Ease Technique is a practice you can use to increase flow, poise and confidence. It can help you significantly reduce your mental and emotional stress when you practice this technique daily. This is not about moving at the speed of a snail, nor is it a sleepy-time relaxation state. Rather, ease is about slowing down what can be called our inner body language – those automatic reactions that cause us to make mistakes, compromise friendships and drain our energy through frustration, impatience or anger.

Shifting to Ease at the Onset of Stress

Learning to shift to a state of inner ease at the onset of challenging situations can help prevent and eliminate many unwanted predicaments. This will make it easier for you to successfully navigate your way through challenges. If you practice it a few times each day for several weeks, it will become a natural part of your daily routine.

College students use Inner-Ease in a variety of ways:

- In the morning to prep for the day

- In between classes or activities

- Transitioning from one event to another

- When frustration, anxiety or impatience with yourself or others comes up

- Waiting in line

- Driving

- Before social interactions

- Before and during long periods of concentrated study

- Before sleep

Steps of the Inner-Ease™ Technique

1. If you are feeling stressed, acknowledge your feelings as soon as you sense that you are out of sync or feeling frustrated, anxious, angry, etc. (*This step can be the hardest because often, our stressful feelings become so automatic that we don't even notice them.*)

2. Next, take a short time-out and do heart-focused breathing: Breathe a little slower and deeper than usual as you imagine breathing through your heart or chest area. (*As with the previous techniques taught in this handbook, this may take a little getting used to, but most people find that with intention and practice, it's easy to shift into heart-centered breathing.*)

3. During your heart-focused breathing, imagine with each breath that you are drawing in a feeling of inner ease or emotional balance. (*Drawing in a feeling of inner ease is like imagining that you are breathing in a pleasant aroma from a bouquet of roses.*)

4. When your stressful feelings have stabilized, affirm with a solid commitment that you want to anchor and maintain the state of ease as you re-engage in your projects, challenges or daily interactions. (*It is OK if a disruption takes you out of the ease state. Simply reset your intention with a genuine commitment and move on.*)

Prep for Maintaining Mental and Emotional Balance

One of the best times to use the Inner-Ease Technique is as a prep before activities, tasks or interactions, especially those likely to be challenging. Prepping is a smart strategy because it helps you stay coherent and balanced. It is the same kind of preparation athletes routinely use just before competition. They know the importance of staying calm and centered, not only to do their best, but also to quickly recover when they make a false start or bad play. Maintaining a state of ease helps sustain a higher level of performance and prevents energy drain. For instance, when golfers hit bad putts, they know if they fail to manage their frustration, it could carry over to the next tee, fairway or green.

How to Prep

- Visualize or project yourself into a future event in which you sense there could be a stressful challenge.

- Take a short time-out and do heart-focused breathing by breathing a little slower and deeper than usual.

- Have the intention of dealing with the situation in a balanced way. (This means not only thinking about ease or calm, but engaging in heart-centered breathing to establish coherence and then imagining yourself maintaining ease and calm in the situation.)

Exercise:

Identify three times during the day when you can practice the Inner-Ease Technique.

1. _____

2. _____

3. _____

After practicing the Inner-Ease Technique 2-3 times a day, what do you notice?

_____

Is it hard? _____ Is it easy? _____

Write about your experience.

_____

_____

_____

_____

_____

> Practicing Inner-Ease creates 'flow' by helping to regulate the balance and cooperation between our heart, mind and emotions. It allows us an extra time-window to discern effective choices, reactions, decisions, and how we respond to life and to others."
>
> — Doc Childre, *The State of Ease*[11]

"People who learn to control inner experience will be able to determine the quality of their lives, which is as close as any of us can come to being happy."

—Mihaly Csikszentmihalyi, *Flow: The Psychology of Optimal Experience, 1990*

Questions to Ponder:

1. Can you think of instances in which you observed individuals, groups or teams being in the zone? What specifically did you notice that indicated they were in the zone?

2. Is being in the zone or experiencing flow an abstract concept to you, or do you have firsthand experience of this state? If so, describe a time when you experienced it.

3. What benefits do athletes receive when using prep before competitive events?

4. Can you identify two areas or situations in which you could apply the Inner-Ease Technique?

Chapter 8

Three Keys for Sustaining Resilience

The techniques and strategies you have learned in this guide are designed to help you take charge of your stressful feelings and experience greater ease and resilience in your busy life. These techniques can become habits if you make it a goal to practice and apply them regularly over the next two to four weeks. You may find that one of the techniques works better for you than another. For some people, it is easier to activate a positive emotion, whereas others might find it easier to generate the state of ease.

> *Prep*, *Sustain* and *Reset*
> Three keys for becoming familiar with the
> state of coherence and making it a habit.

Prep

As discussed in the last chapter, using a self-regulation technique *before* an activity, task or interaction is a smart way to help you stay balanced and coherent, especially in challenging situations. Too often, we crash into the same stressors over and over again, reacting with predictable behavior that sets off a cascade of physiological stress responses. For hours afterward, we carry around stressful feelings such as frustration, anxiety or discouragement that disrupt our focus and inhibit our performance and creativity.

Prepping beforehand with the Inner-Ease or Quick Coherence techniques can prevent a lot of energy drain. Applying these techniques as much as 5 to 10 minutes before an exam, interaction or event, will help you maintain greater ease and calm in any upcoming situation. As you become involved in the activity, casually and discretely reapply the technique, even if you are around other people.

Sustain

When you have a full and demanding schedule, you can stay more coherent and pre-serve your energy and resilience by regularly practicing a technique such as Inner-Ease.

A perfect opportunity for taking a time-out to breathe in a feeling of ease and temporarily clearing your mind from pressing thoughts is when you are going from one class to the next. Many students sched-ule 3 to 5 minutes of quiet practice time in the library to recharge their emotional batteries. If you are headed home from the campus or work, you could take a little time to practice Quick Coherence for several minutes.

Reset

Inevitably, you will have a stress reaction to some event or interaction. It is unavoid-able in today's fast-moving, complex world. When that happens, you can minimize any negative effects by applying a technique like Freeze Frame or Inner-Ease to help calm you down and regain perspective and clarity. As soon as possible after a stress reaction, walk yourself through the steps of the Freeze Frame Technique to reset your initial fight, flight or freeze reaction.

This is similar to rebooting your computer when it is frozen. When you restart your computer, you are attempting to give your operating system a fresh start and clean out the clutter. When you do Heart-Focused Breathing, you are resetting your physi-ology and attempting to reestablish your composure. Some stress reactions will be more dramatic than others and the emotions you experience may take longer to recede, but utilizing these techniques can help you clean out the mental and emotional clutter sooner.

Use this handbook to make coherence and inner ease new familiar states in your life. Take charge of your habitual reactions to the things that stress you and transform them into more intelligent, constructive responses.

Your reward will be a happier, more resilient life, with a lot less energy drain, frustration and fatigue.

Review of Self-Regulation Techniques

Although the techniques taught in this handbook are distinct from one another, there is some overlap in their general purposes. For instance, Quick Coherence and Inner Ease both reduce stress while Freeze Frame and Asset/Deficit aid in decision-making. Create a practice plan using one or more of these techniques that suits your personal needs.

Each of the techniques is summarized below with an overview of functions and applications.

Quick Coherence® Technique

Purpose: Reduce stress and improve resilience.

Quick Coherence Technique Quick Steps:

    1. Heart-Focused Breathing

    2. Activate a positive feeling

Recommended Practice Times

Practicing the Quick Coherence Technique two or three times a day benefits you mentally, emotionally and physically. Areas of application include:

- Driving to school or walking to class
- During stressful times in class
- During a break
- In sporting activities
- Before going to sleep
- Before or during important meetings or other interactions

Inner-Ease™ Technique

Purpose: Create greater poise and flow throughout your day and reduce mental and emotional stress.

Inner-Ease Technique Quick Steps

1. **Acknowledge your feelings**
2. **Heart-focused Breathing**
3. **Draw in a feeling of inner ease**
4. **Anchor and maintain the feeling**

Recommended Practice Times

- In the morning to prep for the day
- When experiencing frustration, anxiety or impatience with yourself or others
- Waiting in line, driving, before social interactions
- Before and during long periods of concentrated study
- Before sleep

Freeze Frame® Technique

Purpose: To promote greater clarity in problem-solving, decision-making and creativity.

The Quick Steps of the Freeze Frame Technique

1. Identify

2. Heart-Focused Breathing

3. Activate

4. Ask/observe

Recommended Applications

- Decision-making

- Problem-solving

- Creative brainstorming

Asset/Deficit Balance Sheet

Purpose: To help promote intelligent decision-making.

The Asset/Deficit Tool Instructions:

1. Write down a decision or problem that you wish to address. Frame this as a yes or no question.
   (Shou*ld I drop my psychology class?)*

2. Write down as many assets (positives) as you can.
   (*There is a history class I would like to take.)*

3. Write down as many deficits (negatives) as you can (*There are too many people in the class.*)

4. As an option, assign one to three points to each entry based on its level of importance. If you assigned points, add up both the assets and deficits and subtract the difference to determine which has the highest point total.

5. After practicing the Freeze Frame Technique for 1 to 2 minutes, ask yourself the question you came up with in No. 1.

6. Review the entries in both the Asset and Deficit columns and write down a conclusion that describes the best choice for you.

Recommended Applications

- Decision-making

- Problem-solving

- Creative brainstorming

Emotional Landscape

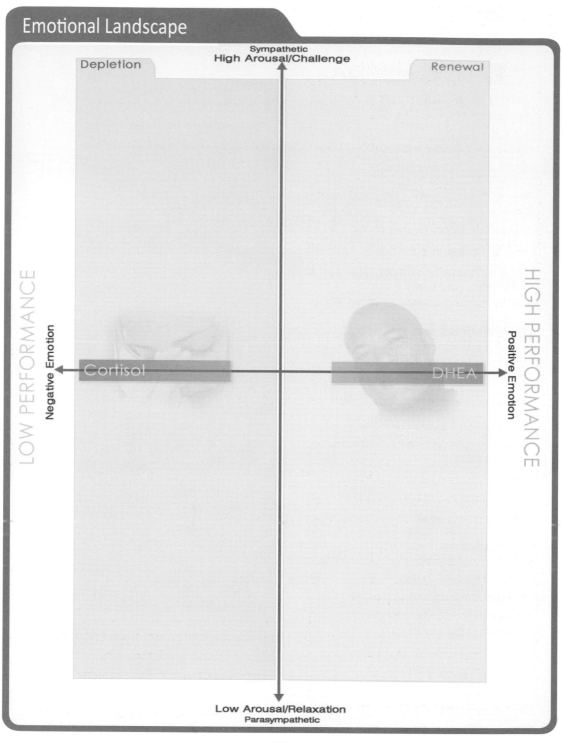

Freeze Frame® Exercise

Step 1: Identify

Identify the problem or issue and any stressful feelings or reactions related to it.

Step 2: Heart-Focused Breathing

Imagine your breath is flowing in and out of your heart area to help you calm down and reduce the intensity of a stress-producing reaction. Take slow, casual deep breaths.

Step 3: Activate

Make a sincere effort to activate a positive feeling.

Step 4: Ask

From a more objective place, ask yourself what would be an efficient, effective attitude, action or solution.

Step 5: Observe

Quietly observe any thoughts, feelings or perceptions that could add clarity to the situation and commit to acting on them.

If no insights come up, that's OK. Repeat the process later or the next day.

Decision/Issue:

_____

Reaction:

_____

_____

_____

Effective Action or Attitude

_____

_____

_____

_____

_____

Often, solutions are inspired through
communicating with
or getting input from others.

This technique is adapted from the original version of Freeze Frame for this book.

Asset/Deficit Balance Worksheet

Part 1: Write down a decision or problem that you wish to address. Frame the decision in the form of a yes or no question. List the assets or positives in one column and the deficits or negatives in the second column.

Decision:_____

Assets	Deficits

Part 2: Once both lists are complete, practice Freeze Frame for 1-2 minutes to help neutralize any bias towards a particular outcome. Then ask yourself what is the most intelligent conclusion you can draw based on the overall information from both columns.

Steps of the Freeze Frame® Technique
- **Identify**
- **Heart-Focused Breathing**
- **Activate**
- **Ask/Observe**

Conclusion:_____

_____

References

Chapter 1

[1] FreeDictionary, Farlex, Inc., retrieved May 9, 2011, from http://www.thefreedictionary.com/stress.

[2] Morrow, A., (2011) retrieved May 9, 2011, from About.com http://dying.about.com/od/glossary/g/stress.html.

[3] *Understanding and Dealing with Stress*, from Mountain State Centers for Independent Living, http://www.mtstcil.org/skills/stress-definition-1.html.

[4] Hansen, R., (2011) *Your First Year of College: 25 Tips to Help You Survive and Thrive Your Freshman Year and Beyond*, retrieved May 9, 2011, http://www.quintcareers.com/first-year_success.html.

[5] American Psychological Association, *Stress a Major Health Problem in The U.S., Warns APA*, Oct. 24, 2007, retrieved May 9, 2011, from http://www.apa.org/news/press/releases/2007/10/stress.aspx.

[6] The American Institute of Stress, *AMERICA'S NO. 1 HEALTH PROBLEM: Why is there more stress today?* Rosch, P., 1991, retrieved May 9, 2011, from http://www.stress.org.

[7] mtvU and Associated Press 2009 poll, *Economy, College Stress and Mental Health*, retrieved May 9, 2011, from http://www.halfofus.com/_media/_pr/may09_exec.pdf.

[8] Ibid.

[9] *Man Health Magazine Online*, adapted from *Jokes about Stress and Humor*, retrieved May 9, 2011, from http://www.man-health-magazine-online.com/joke-stress.html.

[10] Womble, L.P., *Impact of Stress Factors on College Students' Academic Performance*, University of North Carolina, Charlotte, retrieved May 9, 2011, from www.psych.uncc.edu/Womble.pdf.

Chapter 2

[1] Armour, J.A., (1994), *Neurocardiology: Anatomical and Functional Principles*, New York, N.Y., Oxford University Press: 3-19.

[2] McCraty, R., *Heart-brain Neurodynamics: The Making of Emotions*, Boulder Creek, Calif., HeartMath Research Center, Institute of HeartMath (2003). Available as an electronic monograph at: www.heartmath.org.

[3] Ibid.

[4] McCraty, R., Atkinson, M., Tiller, W.A., Rein, G.,Watkins, A.D., *The Effects of Emotions on Short-Term Power Spectrum Analysis of Heart Rate Variability*, American Journal of Cardiology, (1995); 76(14).

Chapter 3

[1] *Should your G.P.A. prevent you from getting your next job?* Posted Sept. 12, 2007 by The Jobs Bloggers, http://microsoftjobsblog.com.

[2] From the article, *Job Outlook: Employers Note Positive Projections in 'Good' Job Market*, posted at http://www.naceweb.org/so11172010/job_outlook_2011/, based on NACE Job Outlook 2011 survey.

[3] Swank, R. L. and W. E. Marchand. (1946) Adapted from *Combat Neuroses: Development of Combat Exhaustion*, Archives of Neurology and Psychiatry, 55:236–47.

[4] *Stressed out? When the college workload kicks your butt*, The Daily Hampshire Gazette, Gazettenet.com, http://www.gazettenet.com/2010/09/06/stressed-out-when-college-workload-kicks-your-butt.

[5] Ibid.

[6] Damasio, A., *Descartes' Error: Emotion, Reason, and the Human Brain*, Putnam Publishing, 1994.

Chapter 4

[1] McCraty, R., & Tomasino, D. (2006), *The Coherent Heart: Heart-brain interactions, Psychophysiological Coherence, and the Emergence of System Wide Order*, Boulder Creek, Calif., HeartMath Research Center, Institute of HeartMath.

[2] Ibid.

[3] Collins, A.B., (2009), *Life experiences and resilience in college students: A relationship influenced by hope and mindfulness,* Ph.D. dissertation, Texas A&M University, Texas Digital Library.

[4] Fredrickson, B., (2001), *Joy and Love Genetically Encoded, Research News and Opportunities* in *Science and Theology.*

[5] Ratanasiripong, P., (2010) *Setting Up the Next Generation Biofeedback Program for Stress and Anxiety Management for College Students: A Simple and Cost-Effective Approach, College Student Journal,* Vol. 44 Nbr. 1, March 2010.

Chapter 5

[1] Ingwersen, J., Defeyter, M.A., Kennedy, D.O., Wesnes, K.A., Scholey, A.B. *A low glycemic index breakfast cereal preferentially prevents children's cognitive performance from declining throughout the morning, Appetite,* July 2007; 49(1):240-4.

[2] Rampersaud, G.C., Pereira, M.A., Girard, B.L., Adams, J., Metzl, J.D., *Breakfast Habits, Nutritional Status, Body Weight, and Academic Performance in Children and Adolescents,* J Am Diet Association. 2005 May; 105(5):743-60;

[3] Vgontzas, A.N., Bixler, E.O., Lin, H.M., Prolo, P., Mastorakos, G., Vela-Bueno, A., Kales, A. and ChrousosChronic GP. *Insomnia Is Associated with Nyctohemeral Activation of the Hypothalamic-Pituitary-Adrenal Axis: Clinical Implications, Journal of Clinical Endocrinology and Metabolism,* August 2001; 86:3787-3794.

[4] Gais, S., Born, J. *Declarative memory consolidation,: mechanisms acting during human sleep, Learning and Memory.* November-December 2004;11(6):679-85.

[5] Brody, J.E., *A Good Night's Sleep Isn't a Luxury; It's a Necessity, New York Times, Science Times,* May 31, 2011, D7.

[6] Ibid.

[7] Mayo Clinic Staff, *10 Tips for Better Sleep from Mayo Clinic,* retrieved May 23, 2011 from

http://www.mayoclinic.com/health/sleep.

[8] Hamilton, J., *Multitasking Brain Divides and Conquers, To a Point,* NPR 15 Aug 2011;, Retrieved 31 May 2011 fromhttp://www.npr.org/templates/story/story.php?storyId=126018694.

[9] Foerde, K., Knowlton, B., *Multi-Tasking Adversely Affects Brain's Learning, Science Daily,* July 26,2006, Retrieved 30 May 2011 from http://www.sciencedaily.com/releases/2006/07/060726083302.htm.

[10] Linda Stone, http://lindastone.net, Continuous Partial Attention.

[11] Ibid.

[12] Stone, L., *Just Breathe: Building the case for Email Apnea, TheHuffingtonPost.com,* Linda Stone, February 8, 2008.

[13] *Hamlet's BlackBerry: To Surf Or Not To Surf,* NPR, *Listen to the Story,* July 20, 2010, retrieved June 6, 2011 from http://www.npr.org/templates/story/story.php?storyId=128364111.

Chapter 6

[1] Oxford University Press, (2010), http://www.oed.com.

[2] Kelci, L., About.com Guide, adapted from *Skills for Time Management for Students,* retrieved from http://collegelife.about.com/od/academiclife/a/Skills-For-Time-Management-For-Students.htm.

[3] Steve Jobs, quoted as saying, *"You've Got to Find What You Love,"* at Stanford University commencement address, June 12, 2005, *Stanford University News,* retrieved June 14, 2005 from 2005june15jobs061505.

Chapter 7

[1] Csikszentmihalyi, M., *Flow: The Psychology of Optimal Experience,* Harper and Row, New York (1990).

[2] Childre,D., *The State of Ease,* http://www.heartmath.org/free-services/downloads/state-of-ease.html.